Saltglaze

CERAMIC SKILLBOOKS

Series Editor:
Murray Fieldhouse

Saltglaze

Peter Starkey

PITMAN

PITMAN PUBLISHING LIMITED
39 Parker Street, London WC2B 5PB

Associated Companies
Copp Clark Ltd, Toronto · Pitman Publishing Corporation/Fearon
Publishers Inc, Belmont, California · Pitman Publishing Co. SA (Pty) Ltd,
Johannesburg · Pitman Publishing New Zealand Ltd, Wellington
Pitman Publishing Pty Ltd, Melbourne

© Pitman Publishing 1977

First published in Great Britain 1977

British Library Cataloguing in Publication Data
Starkey, Peter
    Saltglaze. — (Ceramic Skillbooks).
    1. Pottery craft   2. Glazing (Ceramics)
    I. Title   II. Series
    738.1′2   TT922
    UK ISBN 0-273-01081-6 cased edition
    UK ISBN 0-273-00998-2 paperback edition

Text set in 10/12 pt IBM Century, printed by photolithography and bound
in Great Britain at The Pitman Press, Bath

Contents

Acknowledgements

In compiling this book I am more than conscious that much of the information contained is the outcome of the work of other potters with whom I have been fortunate to be associated. Sharing information was encouraged at Harrow School of Art, where I was the grateful recipient of the experience of earlier students, notably Michelle Docherty, Zelda Mowat, Elenor Epnor and Bill Van Gilder, together with the teaching of Walter Keeler.

My thanks are due to the following for providing photographs, information and recipes: Walter Keeler, John Maltby, Ian Gregory, Jane Hamlyn, University of Wales, Homer Sykes, Max Zwissler, CAC and David Lewis.

Particular thanks to Alan Richmond, my bank manager, for being so understanding.

Preface

I write this book not as an expert, but as an enthusiast. The contents of this book describe methods and techniques which I have used. In no way are they intended to be dogmatic statements or rules about how to saltglaze.

The principle of saltglazing has been known since the fourteenth century and has had a chequered career in its application. Over the years saltglazing has been put to a wide variety of uses, from delicate figurines to sewerage pipes. However, despite its familiarity, and unlike most of the other mediums employed by the studio potter, saltglazing is still a relatively unexplored technique. The opportunity for genuine discovery or re-discovery is multifold. When embarking on saltglazing, the potter has before him, or her, an unlimited opportunity for extending the scope and range of the technique in a very personal way.

There are many variables inherent in saltglazing: the very nature of the method is the use of a vapour, which is not the most controllable of agents. The glazing takes place during the maturation of the clay, at a time in the making process when the influences of the potter can only be indirect. Each kiln seems to behave differently, often giving very unexpected results, even when previously known formulae have been used. The saltglazer's kiln is a very personal piece of equipment.

The methods outlined in this book are ones which I have used to give the kind of results that I wanted. They are by no means definitive of the possibilities open to the potter. The really exciting thing about salting is that the standard of achievement has yet to be set. For me, it is the most exciting way of making pots, often very exasperating, but never dull or predictable. The possibility for consumate elation or depression seems infinite.

Above all else, enjoy salting for its delights, despite the inevitable accompanying disappointments. Opening a kiln might not be quite like Christmas Day (there may be *no* presents!), but the anticipation and excitement at the prospect of the contents is, for me anyway, a recurring pleasure and a spur to further endeavour.

1 Early Saltglaze

The technique of saltglazing was discovered around the 14th century in Europe, probably in Germany, just how is not known. Its most common form was in its application to the making of wine jars and bottles in Germany and Holland, and by the 17th century John Dwight of Fulham was manufacturing salted ware in England.

Salting produces a very hard, well-fitting glaze and has the advantage of not requiring an intermediate biscuit stage. This meant that pottery could be produced more cheaply and quickly than by other methods. Despite a rich period of manufacturing during the early 18th century when many beautiful articles were made at Fulham and in Staffordshire, the technique, because of its economy, was employed almost exclusively for the making of utilitarian, disposable items. With the exception of the Martin Brothers at the end of the 19th century, salting had become the prerogative of the sewer pipe and heavy clayware manufacturers. This is not to say, however, that the simple bottles and crocks made by the thousand are without their charms. Many have very attractive surfaces and forms which are both strong and honest and offer to the modern, more self-conscious potter a lesson in sound craftmanship and fitness to purpose. Many of these items can still be bought very cheaply and offer a point of reference for anyone interested in salting.

Technical principles
The basic principle of salting is very simple. Salt ($2NaCl$) is thrown into the kiln during the firing at a temperature when the clay is maturing. The salt and the clay ($SiO_2 Al_2O_3$) combine on the surface

of the pot, thereby forming the glaze. Put more simply, the salt vapourizes with the heat at about 1260°C and passes through the pots. The gas contains sodium, which is a flux, and this melts the silicon in the clay, forming the glaze.

For those who enjoy such things, below is a diagram of the chemical reaction.

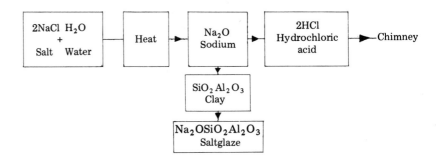

The nature and quality of the glaze is determined by the type of clay from which the pot is made. This can be modified by the use of slips composed of different clays. However, the first prerequisite of the salt-potter is a suitable clay body.

Clay is composed of varying proportions of silica, alumina and fluxes. The salting process is principally concerned with the combination of silica and sodium. Silica is a glass former which, when melted by the fluxing sodium in the salt vapour, forms the glaze. Alumina also plays its part in the reaction to form a sodium-alumino-silicate. The silica in the clay is most active when vitrification temperature is reached. Providing this takes place at a temperature high enough for salt to melt, saltglazing may be successfully employed through a wide range of temperatures.

The amount of silica, alumina and iron in the clay, the temperature of firing, and the methods of salting, all govern the final results. The desired effects are the prerogative of the individual potter to determine. The following information outlines certain basic principles — what is good or bad salting is for the potter to decide.

Fig. 1.1 Figure, white saltglazed stoneware. It is inscribed 'Lydia Dwight died March 3rd, 1673.' This is a portrait of his daughter made by John Dwight, Fulham 1673.

Fig. 1.2 Jug, brown saltglazed stoneware with pierced and incised decoration. This was made at Nottingham
in 1703. The height is 4 inches.

Fig. 1.3 Figure of a monkey with a young one. Saltglazed stoneware made in Staffordshire about 1740. The height is $7\frac{1}{2}$ inches.

5

Fig. 1.4 Mug of saltglazed stoneware with 'scratch-blue' decoration. This was made in Staffordshire in 1752. German beer mugs made today still use the same technique and have the same finish on them as this did over 200 years ago.

Fig. 1.5 This is one of a set of seven plates. It is again saltglazed stoneware and is painted in blue on the rims and in red on the middle. The illustrations on each plate are different and each one recounts one of the Aesop's Fables. These plates are English and were made in Staffordshire about 1760. Each plate is 9 inches in diameter.

Fig. 1.6 Basket, saltglazed earthenware. This is English and dates from
1760. The length from left to right
is $12\frac{1}{2}$ inches.

8

Fig. 1.7 *Top*, this is a block for a plaster mould of a teapot. It is made from saltglazed earthenware. *Left*, the teapot and cover is saltglazed stoneware moulded in relief and painted in colours with portraits of George III and Queen Charlotte. If you look closely at this and the block above you can see that it was made from the latter. The pot on the right is similar to that on the left and they both date from about 1761 and were made in Staffordshire.

10

Fig. 1.8 *Far left*: Jug, saltglazed stoneware by Charles Meigh. This was made at Hanley in 1842. Height $10\frac{1}{8}$ inches.

Fig. 1.9 *Left*: A figure of an owl in saltglazed stoneware made by the Martin Brothers of Southall in 1899. The height is $10\frac{1}{2}$ inches.

Fig. 1.10 *Overleaf*: Jug, modelled with a face on either side, in salt-glazed stoneware by the Martin Brothers of Southall in 1900.

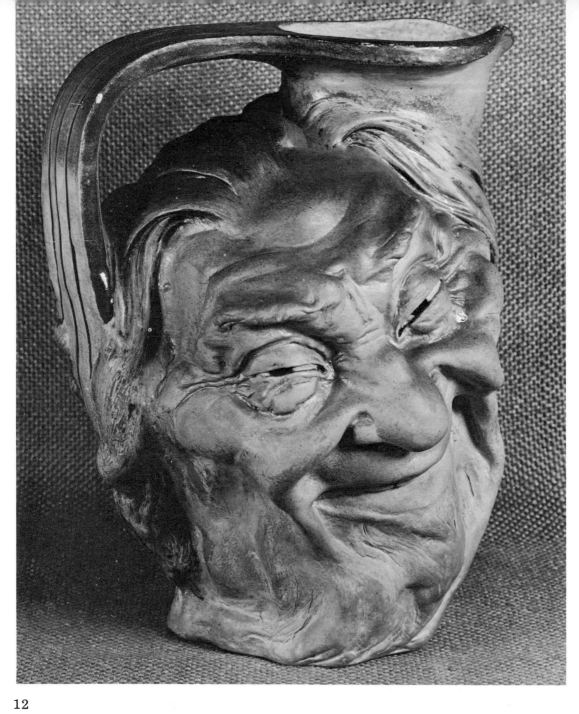

12

2 Basic Principles of Saltglazing

Saltglaze pots are fired in the kiln in the conventional way but they are not glazed before being packed, nor do they need to be biscuited before glaze firing. The clay is put into the kiln in its raw state or, if wished, in biscuit form, and the glazing actually takes place during the firing. Rock salt is thrown into the kiln at around 1260°C and the silica in the clay is fluxed by the sodium in the salt. The sodium vapour attacks the surface of the pots causing the silica to melt and form a glaze on the outside of the clay.

The principal advantage of saltglazing in industry is that it eliminates one whole firing process since pots do not have to be glazed before being set in the kiln, and the need to biscuit does not, therefore, arise. This also appeals to a lot of studio potters as a very direct and economical way of making pots. I prefer to biscuit my pots first, however, because in this way I can apply slips (a thin mix of clay and water) to the pots in a raw state, and also, after biscuit, apply glazes which would not normally adhere to a raw pot. I biscuit to about 1000°C, bearing in mind that as the clays for salting tend to be quite high in silica, it is advisable to biscuit fire a little higher than for a normal firing.

For those who enjoy them, the chemical formulae are listed on page 2. The main active components of saltglazing, as noted above, are sodium and silica. All clays contain some degree of silica and it is from this glass former that the glaze derives. Alumina is the refractory element of the clay which does not react with the sodium at all. Clays vary in their ratios of alumina and silica: the higher the proportion of silica to alumina, the brighter the glaze will be. Obviously the salt potter must know which clay will give him the result he wants. It should be remembered that some clays will not withstand the temperature required to saltglaze. Most earthenware clays, for example, will bloat and deform around $1188°C$ to $1200°C$ and will not give a conventional saltglaze, although they can be salted within a lower temperature range with very interesting results.

Besides the silica content, the iron content of the clay must also be considered. All clays contain iron whether in minute amounts or quite high percentages: a red clay contains 9 per cent iron. Since iron does not attract the salt, in fact it almost resists it, the iron content of the clay is very important. There is a complicated interaction between the silica content of the clay, the iron content, and the temperature to which the clay is fired. The tables on page 46 indicate how the colour of the clay and the brightness of the glaze are affected when the iron content and the temperature are varied. None of these factors can be seen in isolation. The suitability of a particular clay also depends on the kiln atmosphere, that is, whether or not the kiln is reduced or oxidized. Reducing exacerbates the problem of a dull or dark surface in a clay containing too much iron. Strict oxidation, on the other hand, can make an otherwise dark clay more acceptable. For a more detailed discussion of these effects see Chapter 4.

Saltglazing is an inherently variable process. The variables arise principally from the kiln atmosphere, the way in which the salt passes through the kiln, and from the effect of residual salt left in the kiln from previous firings. Because the salting process reduces the kiln, there are many vapours floating about, sometimes very dense, sometimes almost non-existent, with the result that the atmosphere, which governs the colour of the pots, is constantly changing. The residual salt melts each time the kiln is fired and contributes to the overall salting. This means that the kiln is self-salting; once you start to fire you cannot control the salting, because the residual salt is melting all the time. And since the sodium in the residual salt has already combined with the silica in the bricks of the kiln, it is not just sodium, but sodium silicate that is melting. It is much more beneficial to surround the pots with a vapour of total saltglaze. Thus, a broken-in kiln, one that has been well salted with a good coating of glaze throughout, will give a much richer effect for much less salt, than a new kiln, or a kiln built of materials which do not readily absorb the salt. This is discussed in greater detail in Chapter 3.

The relationships between the iron oxide in clay, the silica content and the temperature to which it is fired were explored in 1948 by the Borax company of the United States. This company commissioned several scientists to make a study of the chemical nature of saltglazing in an attempt to establish a standardized method of producing industrial heavy clay ware. Their main concern was to produce smooth, well-coated sewer pipes, tiles and sanitary ware, with a suitable surface conforming to the standards of industry. Barringer, Schurecht and Mackler discovered that the relationship between silica and temperature could be altered very drastically by the amount of iron oxide included. When the kiln was fired to 1145°C Barringer found that if the ferric oxide in the clay body was reduced by 1 per cent, this gave the same brightness of surface as would have resulted from a 7·8 per cent increase in silica. In other words, the less iron in the clay, the brighter the surface became. He later found that if the kiln was fired to 1210°C the 1 per cent reduction of iron oxide was equal to a 12·6 per cent increase in silica. Therefore the higher the kiln was fired, the brighter the result obtained by reducing the iron oxide. It can thus be concluded that the paler the clay, the brighter the resulting surface will be.

If the free silica in the clay is increased to facilitate glazing, the clay may form unstable quartz crystals when cooling and shatter when removed from the kiln. Reducing the iron content of the clay makes an adjustment which is the equivalent of increasing the silica without running the risk of shattering. For instance, porcelain clay, which is highly siliceous and completely free of iron, will give a very smooth uncrazed surface. Red clay which contains 9 to 10 per cent of ferric oxide, hardly glazes at all, giving a dull, almost black metallic surface. The studio potter can exploit these different reactions, perhaps finding a new range of expression, or exploration, by interspersing clays which salt well with clays that do not salt at all. This is most evident in the use of slips; the pot can be coated with a whole range of different coloured slips and with varying degrees of silica.

3 Kilns

The principal requirement for salting is a live flame kiln which uses a fuel such as wood, oil or gas. It is essential to have a live flame because other types of kilns, such as an electric kiln with metal elements, will be immediately damaged by the salt. Down-draught kilns work best for salting as they give a better vapour distribution throughout the ware. The fact that the effluent gases are dangerous to inhale, together with the need for plenty of draught, make it important that the kiln has a good chimney and is sited out of doors.

Heavy firebrick must be used for the main structure of the kiln; a porous insulating brick is not suitable, since the salt attacks not only the pots but the kiln structure itself. Every time the kiln is fired, the inside of the chamber and the kiln furniture, as well as the pots themselves, are glazed, therefore a brick structure which will withstand the pernicious attack of salt vapour is essential. The denser the bricks, the less they will be attacked by the salt. As stated in Chapter 2, the main constituent which combines with the salt is silica. Therefore, the more aluminous the materials from which the kiln is built, the less damage will be caused by the salt and the longer the kiln's life will be. Bricks containing at least 42 per cent alumina, such as Stein's Nettle D bricks or Gibbon's Atlas A2 bricks, should be used whenever possible in the structure. A very high alumina refractory cement from which whole sections of the kiln can be cast will also be very durable. Another material from which refractory structures are made is silicon carbide; this too is very salt resistant and stands up well to attack from slag and gases.

The building of a salt kiln presents a fundamental dilemma in that before a kiln really salts well and gives the results that you want, it must absorb a covering of salt and in doing so begins an inevitable deterioration. Until the interior of the kiln is well salted-up and almost saturated, it will be drawing away the salt from the pots. A kiln has to be broken-in to get the best results. However, of course, from the first firing one is destroying the kiln. The irony of the situation is that just as the pots are firing really well the kiln is fast on its way to falling down. The older the kiln, the more salt it will have in it and the richer the results will be. The obvious temptation is to salt the kiln as rapidly as possible to get good results quickly, but by doing this one merely precipitates the date of the kiln's collapse.

If instead, the kiln is built of very high alumina bricks and refractories then it seldom saturates with salt and is never broken in. The result will be a very long-lasting kiln but the pots, of course, will not be as rich as they could be. The choice is between a short-lived kiln giving good results and a long-lasting kiln producing mediocre pots.

However, a compromise can be reached by building those parts of the kiln which break down soonest from materials with a high alumina content and the rest of the kiln, which is less likely to be damaged, from materials which will give good service and will salt-up well. The diagrams on p. 18 explain which parts of the kiln break down quickly and which parts remain more or less intact. In Fig. 3.1 the areas of maximum damage are shown with a suggestion for the types of materials which will save too rapid wear on the kiln. The principal areas of damage are in the troughs or fireboxes immediately in front of the burners. This is the area in which the salt actually melts and consequently where the bricks break down most rapidly. Unfortunately, since they are also the foundations of all the walls and the floor of the kiln, they are very difficult to replace. If these areas are built from a substance containing as much alumina as possible, then the upper reaches of the walls can be built out of a more conventional type of brick which will salt well and require the minimum amount of maintenance.

Figs. 3.2, 3.3 and 3.4 show how the various parts can be built. Fig. 3.2 shows how a lining of castable alumina can be made on the first two or three courses of the wall, on the base of the firebox and the bagwall. This can also be done on the area immediately in front of the burners: in Fig. 3.2 the end of the wall

Fig. 3.1 *Right*: The textured areas show where maximum wear takes place when using a kiln for salt-glazing, principally in the fire boxes and bagwalls. If you look at Fig. 3.5 you can see exactly what has happened to these areas. They're almost unrecognizable.

Fig. 3.2 *Below*: The shaded part of this fire box can be made of castable alumina in order to protect the very structure of the kiln from deterioration when salting. The wall actually facing the burner will quickly break down unless it is rendered with castable alumina. This should be done whenever possible.

Fig. 3.3 *Opposite*: This diagram shows all the main internal faces of a kiln. The internal walls are made of heavy firebrick and can be covered with a thin coating of alumina batwash.

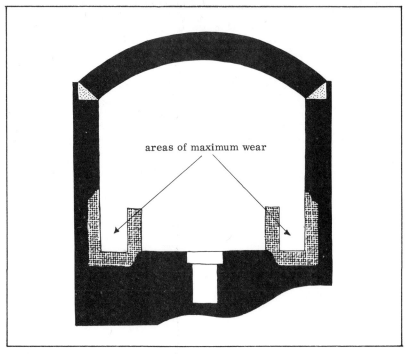

areas of maximum wear

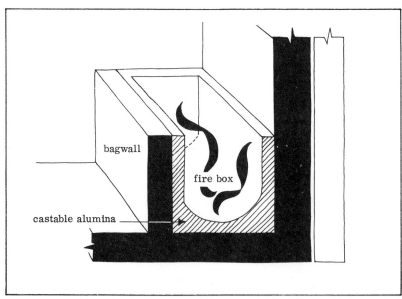

bagwall

fire box

castable alumina

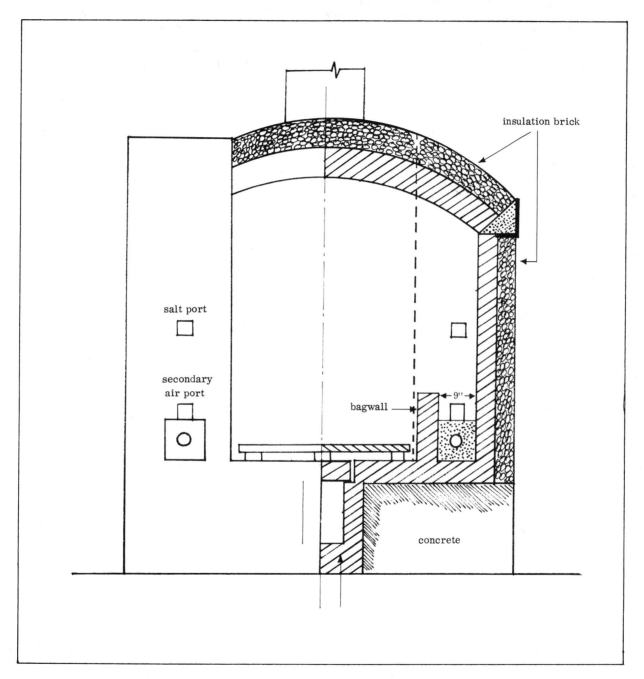

salt port

secondary
air port

bagwall

9"

insulation brick

concrete

19

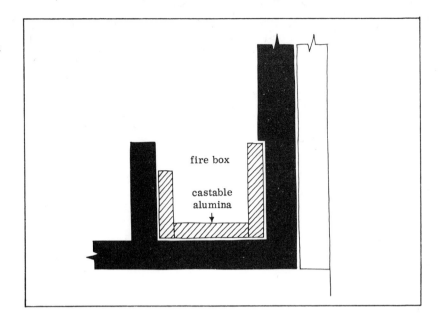

Fig. 3.4 The shaded area represents mortar that can be built into an existing brick wall. Details are given below.

fire box

castable alumina

facing the burner will break down very rapidly unless made of castable alumina. Fig. 3.3 shows how a thinner coating or a trough of castable is merely trowelled on to the existing brick-work. This will break down more rapidly than a lining but can easily be chipped out and replaced when worn. Fig. 3.4 shows how the mortar can be let into the existing brick wall. A rebate is made to take this skin of cement. Tiles can be cast and inserted. The mortar will break down after a while but is easy to chip out and replace. Without this, bagwalls very rapidly collapse and the first couple of courses very soon start to disintegrate. The base of the wall which began as $4\frac{1}{2}$ inches can end up as little as 2 inches thick. The whole of the trough fills up with a mixture of melted brick and salt giving very good results. But by this stage, just when the pots are coming out as you like them, the kiln may be dangerous to fire. It is not only unstable, but because the walls have become thinner the insulatory capacity of the bricks is reduced. The disintegrating brickwork allows the gases to pass through to attack the soft insulating brick on the outer skin of the kiln.

The simplest way to save wear on the kiln is to use kiln-wash. This is a mixture of alumina and a slightly plastic material with a

Fig. **3.5** *Left*: This shows exactly what happens to the structure of a fire box and bagwall after vicious attack from salt. The walls have got thinner and thinner and finally collapsed into the fire box together with a lot of other broken pieces of brick work. As you can see the very foundations of this kiln are beginning to crumble. This can be prevented or at least slowed down to some extent by following the instructions given in Figure 3.2.

Fig. **3.6** *Below*: This is the inside of a fairly new salt kiln at Harrow College of Art. It has been coated with a high alumina batwash which prevents the brick work shelves and kiln props from salting up.

high alumina content, such as china clay (in a proportion of about 3 to 1), is painted like whitewash over the inside of the kiln. In my own work I prefer to encourage the salt to form on most of the kiln and reserve the kiln-wash for those areas where I want the maximum amount of salt resistance to give a longer life.

Kiln designs

As a general rule, the simpler the design, the better. Most kiln designs will work for salt, though down-draught kilns seem to distribute heat and salt more effectively than cross or up-draught kilns. A basic cube is an efficient shape for a smallish kiln such as most studio potters are likely to use. In industry round kilns are used because this shape can take the maximum amount of ware and can be evenly heated. Small-scale round kilns are very difficult to build with rectangular bricks. Oil, gas, wood or coal all work very successfully for salting. Most of my own experience is with oil, although I have also used propane gas. An efficient system of evacuating the gases is essential. There must be a really good chimney to pull the gases through and get rid of them. A high chimney tends to pull the gases into the atmosphere at a

Fig. 3.7 This salt kiln is far away from the house and is inside a very rough shack which will keep any really rough weather away from the burners, blowers and of course the potter.

greater velocity and this speeds dissipation. With a short chimney the gases evacuate slowly and tend to settle over the kiln area.

Since the effluent from the kiln is toxic and has a very damaging effect on metal, to site a salt kiln in a built-up area would be, to say the least, anti-social. It is essential, however, to site it out of doors because working in an enclosed space with salt vapour might damage the lungs. Kiln effluent has not, in my experience, caused any damage to plants or trees.

Kiln furniture

Most saltglaze potters prefer to use carborundum or silicon carbide kiln shelves which are very salt resistant. They are, however, very expensive, costing about three times as much as conventional high alumina kiln shelves. Although they might be expected to give a correspondingly longer service, I have found in practice that they do not justify the additional expense. Since the conventional props used in kilns tend to break down very rapidly, I prefer to use soap bricks which are 3 in. square and 9 in. long. A brick supplier will saw these up into whatever lengths are required. They give extra stability and resist the salt much better than the conventional forms of kiln furniture.

Kiln diagrams

Fig. 3.8 is a plan of a small salt kiln. Very simple to build, it is a fairly standard design for a down-draught kiln. In this case it is oil-fired but it can be modified very simply for gas. Each firebox is 9 in. wide to a 3 in. bagwall, giving a packing space about 27 in. wide which accommodates a 24 in. wide shelf. There is a gap on either side to allow the gases to pass underneath the shelves. The burners are diagonally opposed and give a good circulation of heat. The front burner feeds the back while the back burner feeds the front of the kiln. The bagwalls which force the flames up the chamber walls are two to five courses high. The flames are pulled down through the setting underneath the shelves into the flue, and then out into a 9 in. by 9 in. chimney base running into the chimney which is about 15 ft to 18 ft high.

In the base of the chimney is a damper which plays an important part in the salting process. When closed it reduces the pull of the chimney and the salt vapour stays in the kiln, acting on the

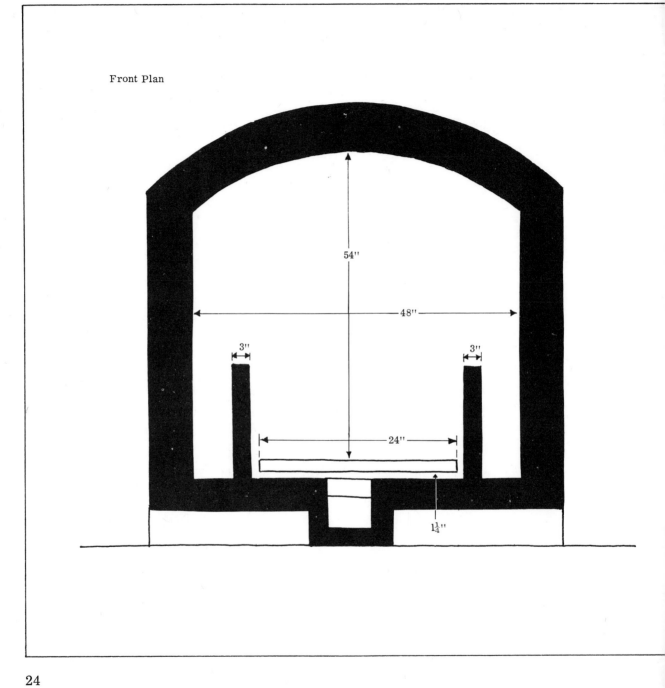

Front Plan

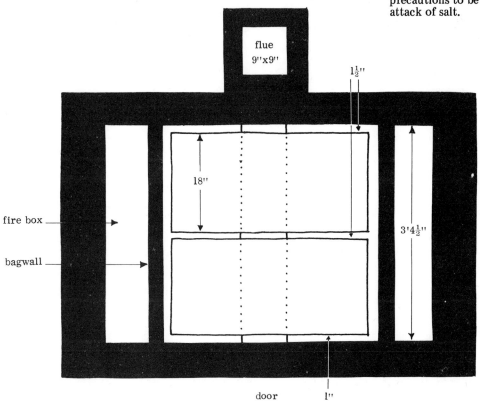

flue
9"x9"

$1\frac{1}{2}$"

18"

$3'4\frac{1}{2}$"

fire box

bagwall

door   1"

Fig. 3.8 These are all the dimensions you will need to put together a small salt kiln. This can be fired by oil or gas. Special precautions when building this kiln will need to be taken to make sure its life is as long as possible. This means intelligent use of castable alumina in the fire boxes and other precautions to be taken against the attack of salt.

pots that much longer. The salt ports are situated immediately above the burners; they are $4\frac{1}{2}$ in. by 3 in. holes in which a brick is placed. The brick can be removed and a packet of salt thrown in. This kiln fires from cold to cone 10 ($1300°$C) in about fourteen hours, using about forty gallons of diesel oil.

If the kiln is adapted for gas, the bagwalls can be placed closer to the walls of the kiln, as gas (which is already vapour) needs less space than oil to combust. The burners are placed in the side walls directly at right angles to them, thus creating more packing space. Oil has to be vaporized before combustion is possible and a great deal of space is required for this. Gas, however, can be bombarded straight against a bagwall and is directed by this obstructing wall up into the chamber. All kilns tend to be rather more wasteful of space if the combustion zones are within the chamber itself.

Fig. 3.9 shows a kiln in which the burners are placed to one side with the combustion zone in a separate little chamber at the side of the kiln. This means that less of the packing area is lost to the combustion zone. With a cross-draught the flames come from one side of the kiln across the chamber into a flue on the opposite side. This system works quite well for salting but gives a less even result than the type of kiln shown in Fig. 3.8. The flame path in this kiln is strongly directional: the vapours rise up the flame channel through the ware from one direction only. Consequently one side of the pots tends to be more heavily salted than the other. Some areas of the kiln will get the full blast and the maximum velocity of the flame while the remainder will have a much gentler heat. The kiln in Fig. 3.8 will give a more even, possibly more predictable result than the cross-draught kiln. One of the requirements of any kiln is a reasonable evenness of temperature, and the cross-draught type can be difficult to fire evenly throughout. There is a tendency to over-fire at the top, long before the bottom of the kiln has reached temperature. Therefore one has to tolerate more extremes of temperature in firing this kiln. More pots can be packed into a cross-draught kiln than into a down-draught kiln and the more dramatic effects resulting from the flame and salt bath can be very desirable.

The kiln shown in Fig. 3.10 is basically the same as that in Fig. 3.8 except that it has been adapted for firing with wood. Wood is a bulky fuel and obviously requires much more space to

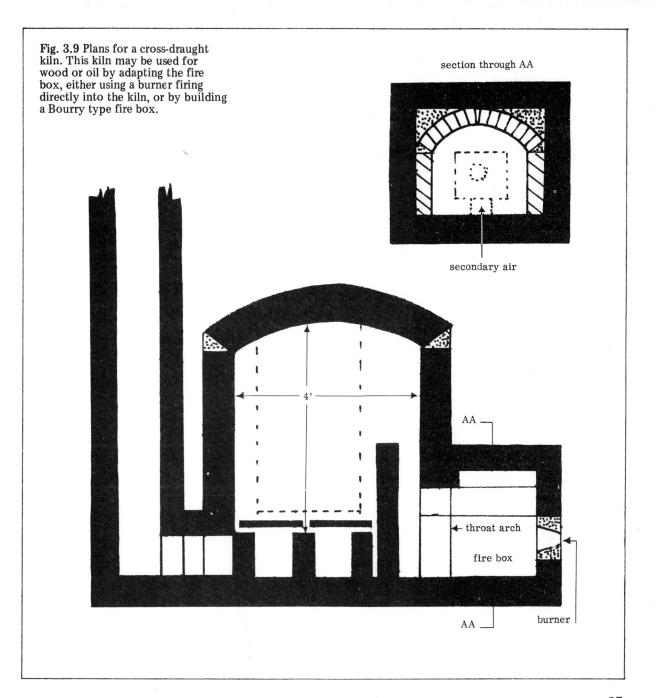

Fig. 3.9 Plans for a cross-draught kiln. This kiln may be used for wood or oil by adapting the fire box, either using a burner firing directly into the kiln, or by building a Bourry type fire box.

section through AA

secondary air

AA

throat arch

fire box

AA

burner

4'

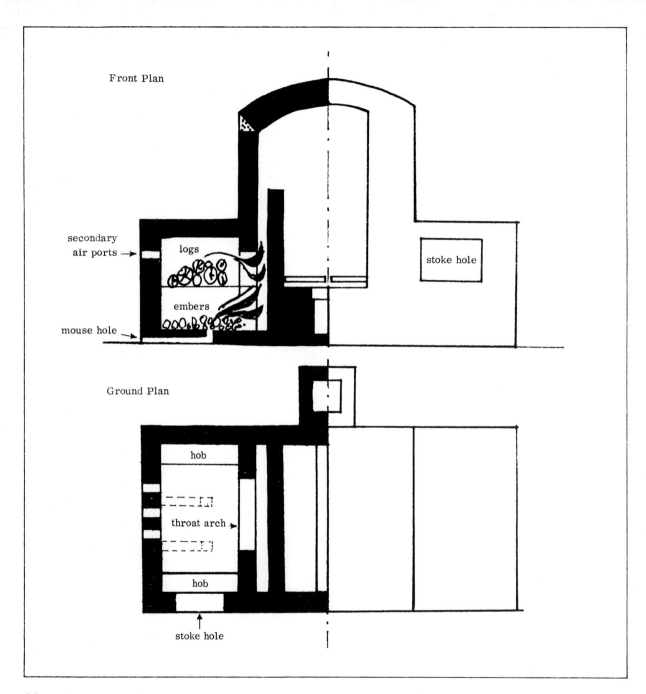

Front Plan

secondary
air ports →

logs

stoke hole

embers

mouse hole →

Ground Plan

hob

throat arch →

hob

stoke hole

28

combust. Each firebox is placed on one side of the kiln. The wood flame is very long and can pass from the firebox right through the kiln and up the chimney. It has some advantages over oil and gas. It requires no machinery in the way of burners. It is silent, it smells much nicer and is more fundamentally appealing than the other fuels. This particular kiln has Bourry type fireboxes which give a very efficient fuel consumption with a minimum amount of stoking. The flames, as in a down-draught kiln, pass up both sides of the kiln giving a good heat distribution.

The salt in this kiln is introduced on top of the burning embers in the firebox. This means that the fly ash (the ashes of the wood, released each time the kiln is stoked) is pulled through the kiln together with the gases. Ash is a very important flux which has long been used in the making of glazes. Many Korean and Chinese glazes, for example, use wood ash as a flux. The addition of another flux besides sodium introduces another variable to the already unpredictable process.

Wood gives a particularly fine quality of reduction. The atmosphere inside a kiln very much affects the colour of the glazes, slips and clay in the kiln. Each time it is stoked a cloud of black smoke passes through the kiln. As this settles down there is a period of oxidation and a good clean flame. This is a natural oxidizing and reducing cycle. Add this to the salt, and there is a much varied (and still less predictable) series of reactions taking place. Certainly the richest effects in salting tend to come from wood firing, so while wood is a more risky method of firing, it is more rewarding. The rewards, of course, tend to be greatest when the most is likely to be lost.

All these kilns have been constructed basically on the same principle, that of a cube with a sprung arch. Fig. 3.11 shows another style altogether: the catenary arch kiln. The shape of the arch is arrived at very simply by hanging a chain from two nails spaced, say, three feet apart. If the resulting curve is traced and then inverted it gives the catenary arch shape. From an engineering point of view this particular arch is very valuable to the kiln builder as it is self-supporting. The natural tendency of sprung arches is to collapse because the forces of the arch are lateral: on a catenary arch the nature of the curve is such that the forces are down the walls into the ground. This type of arch does not require supporting. Other kiln arches have to be held together with iron bracing. With a catenary arch kiln all you

Fig. 3.10 *Opposite*: A wood fired kiln. Here the fire boxes obviously need care and attention in their construction. This is a simplified drawing of a wood firing kiln suitable for saltglazing. The fire boxes are of the Bourry type which work by burning logs across hobs. When burnt the embers fall into an ashpit below, where, with the aid of heated air from the mousehole, they form charcoal that gives off radiated heat that passes through the throat arch into the kiln. This, with the long flames from the wood above, distribute heat very efficiently throughout the kiln chamber. A more detailed drawing of this type of fire box can be seen in Michael Cardew's *Pioneer Pottery*, Longmans, 1969.

Fig. 3.11 A Catenary kiln. The inner layer of the arch should be made from hard fabric and the outer layer from insulating brick. The internal chamber depth here is 3 ft 4½ inches and the shelf size is 24 inches by 18 inches by 1¼ inches.

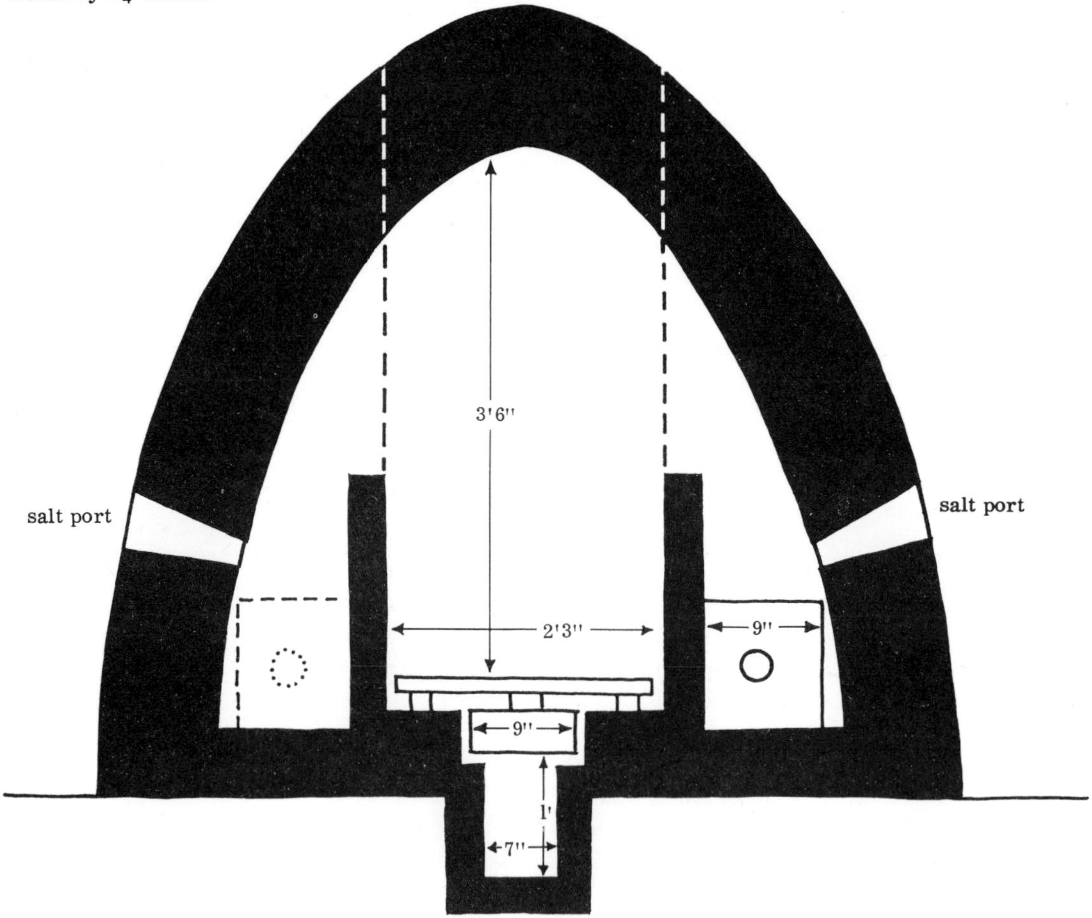

salt port

salt port

3'6"

2'3"

9"

9"

1'

7"

need to do is to make a former out of wood, build bricks over the former and simply slide it out when set, leaving the kiln standing up on its own and requiring no further bracing. Because the resulting chamber is narrower at the top, packing space is reduced, but this is more than compensated for by the fact that it is much simpler to build and is in itself a beautiful shape. This kiln can be fired with wood, oil or gas by adapting the size of the fireboxes. I have found that it works best with oil burners placed in the front and back. If it is to be used with gas, the bagwalls can be moved in slightly and gas burners put in the side.

A catenary kiln can be dismantled when it is old much more quickly than a conventional kiln. All you need to do, in fact, is turn it inside out. In the first three kilns there is a lot of space in which the flames can combust, and in which the salt can pass from the fireboxes into the chamber. Because of the sloping walls of the catenary kiln, the fireboxes get narrower as they get taller. The expanding gases have less room in which to expand, so there is a restriction between the bagwall and the wall of the chamber immediately above. In the case of a small kiln, a bagwall need only be one or two bricks high and so the restriction is not very important, but on bigger kilns it can be a problem. There is a tendency to have too much salt jamming up in this area, because the area above the bagwall is restricting, so the pots along this side tend to be over-salted. As the sides of the kiln restrict the draughts, too little salt reaches the top of the chamber and too much at the sides and the bottom. This can be compensated for by reducing the size of the shelves as they go up the kiln. In this way the same distance all the way around the side is maintained. As with the cross-draught kiln, however, this characteristic can also be turned to advantage by the appropriate placing of slips, glazes, or pots on which extremes of colour or texture are desired.

Kiln building is an art rather than a science, and is not disposed to conventional rules or formulae of proportion. However some basic rules of thumb may be applied.

1 Build the size of kiln which is right for you.
2 Make sure that the required kiln shelves are available or, better still, build your kiln with the bottom shelves in place, to be sure they fit.
3 A cube is a good starting point for the chamber.

4 Fireboxes for oil should be about 9 in. wide, and 24 in. to 27 in. to the first obstruction from the flame.

5 Leave at least one inch between kiln shelves and the floor of the kiln.

6 Avoid making the kiln too tall.

7 Make flues larger than needed: they can easily be restricted later. Flues that are too small can be difficult to alter.

8 Build a high chimney, at least four times the internal chamber height.

Fig. 3.12 *Far left*: View of a kiln showing the burner system, in this case oil. The blowers are simply old vacuum cleaners piped up to the burner mechanisms. Photo: Homer Sykes.

Fig. 3.13 *Left*: Walter Keeler's salt kiln shows how salt has run off the bricks that made up the door at the bottom right of this picture. This is because they were coated with a very high alumina batwash, and salt did not attack the brickwork. Some of the pots that came from this kiln can be seen on top of it. The chain across the middle is purely structural.

Fig. 3.14 *Above*: Jane Hamlyn's salt kiln is packed and the door is about to be bricked up before firing.

Fig. 3.15 These are plans for John
Maltby's salt kiln.

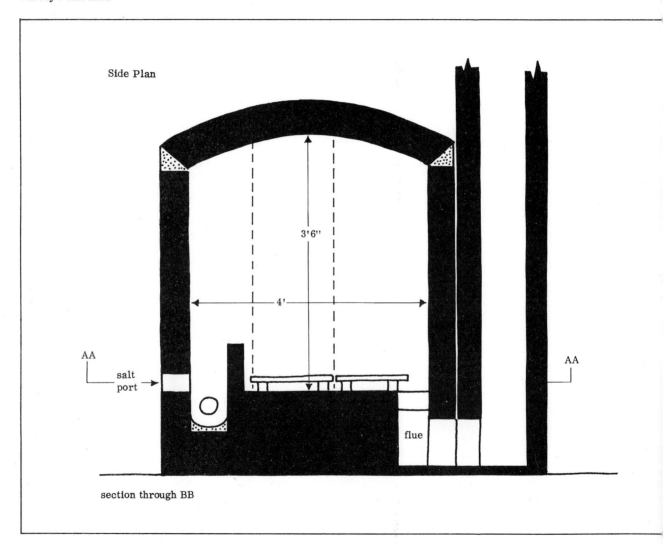

Side Plan

3'6"

4'

AA

salt
port

AA

flue

section through BB

section through AA   Ground Plan

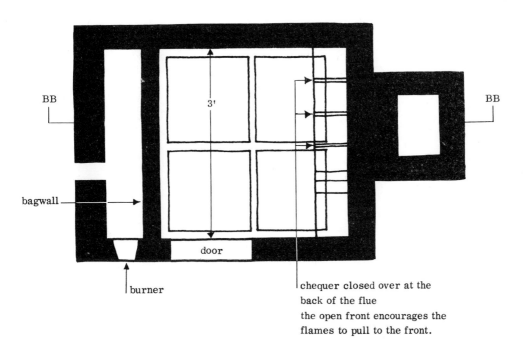

BB

bagwall

burner

3'

door

chequer closed over at the
back of the flue
the open front encourages the
flames to pull to the front.

BB

4 Firing a Salt Kiln

This schedule for an oil firing is for pots which have already been biscuited and does not therefore include the preliminary period of very slow firing in order to drive off the chemical water in the clay. The kiln can rise fairly rapidly in temperature throughout the firing. In this case I turn the burners on at about 7 o'clock in the morning, having packed the kiln the day before. The burners are turned on gently at first to warm up the kiln. Oil will not burn efficiently until the firebox in the front of the kiln is fairly hot. If everything is going well, then by 10.30 a.m. the kiln is reading about 960°C, a fairly rapid heat rise. (Some burners will not do this: certain very sophisticated ones will not atomize the fuel quickly enough to give this heat rise. The reader must bear in mind that this particular schedule is based entirely on the working of my own kiln and the burners I use.) By about 12 o'clock, 1060°C has been reached, and at this point I start to reduce the kiln. Reducing the kiln is simply cutting off the supply of excess oxygen to the kiln itself and therefore to the flame which passes into the kiln. Anything that burns requires oxygen to do so; starving the flame of oxygen by sealing ports in which air can travel into the kiln causes the flame to take oxygen from wherever it can — in this case, principally from the clay and the glazes in the pots. Oxygen is drawn from the oxides in the pots and reduces them back to their original state, radically altering the final appearance of the ware.

I reduce by simply closing off the secondary air ports (the primary air in the kiln is the air which passes in through the burner from the blowers which atomizes the oil). Secondary air is any other air which is allowed to pass into the kiln. In order to keep

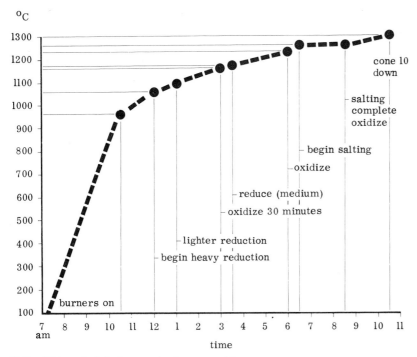

°C

Fig. 4.1 A salt kiln schedule. This graph shows the rise in temperature against the time. This is by no means exactly what should happen, but the behaviour of temperature and the approximate times for salting do give a useful working guide.

cone 10
down

salting
complete
oxidize

– begin salting

–oxidize

– reduce (medium)

– oxidize 30 minutes

– lighter reduction

– begin heavy reduction

burners on

7   8   9   10   11   12   1   2   3   4   5   6   7   8   9   10   11
am

time

N.B.   This schedule is meant only as a guide

the atmosphere inside clean, secondary air ports are provided. These consist of loose bricks above the burner ports which can be removed to allow air to enter. I close these over, and leave the primary air and the oil as it is. This causes the atmosphere in the kiln to become hazy and smoky. Some people prefer to put a damper into the base of the chimney; this restricts the pull of the chimney, causing pressure to build up in the chamber. If the pull of the chimney is restricted, eventually the gases produced by the flame will not be able to evacuate as quickly as the other gases coming in, and a very smoky atmosphere results. The new fuel which is coming in will not combust properly and there will be fine droplets of carbon and oil in the kiln atmosphere causing incomplete combustion. This is fairly heavy in the early stages and by 1 o'clock, an hour later, when the kiln has got to about 1100°C, I lessen the reduction a little. When the flames are not combusting efficiently, the temperature rise is that much slower. If reduction is too heavy, the kiln does not rise in tem-

perature and fuel is wasted. I like to alternate between a heavy
reduction which has the most effect on the pots, and a light
reduction which helps to get the temperature up. In a way this
simulates natural oxidation and reduction as in a wood firing
and it seems to give more interesting results.

At 3 o'clock, the 1160 cone is starting to go over and the
residual salt is beginning to melt and vaporize. The kiln is
oxidized by opening the secondary air ports, making the atmosphere as clean as possible. There is a very good reason for this.
The principle of reduction is a curious one, in that it alters the
colour of the clay and the glazes, but this reduction is not evident
until the clay has been re-oxidized. If the clay is reduced and
cooled instantly without being oxidized it is a dull grey colour.
If, however, reduction is followed by oxidation the colour is
warm, rich and attractive.

Once the clay is vitrified, gases can no longer pass through the
body of the pot. If a pot which is completely oxidized or reduced
is put back into the kiln and fired again after vitrification, no
amount of oxidizing or reducing will have any effect. The salt
evaporates by 1160°C, therefore the pots are starting to take salt
and become sealed. To continue to reduce at this stage would
be to risk sealing the reduction into the pot and grey and
uninteresting surfaces would result.

Having oxidized the kiln for thirty minutes, I then reduce it
again. If the pot is, in fact, sealed, then this further reduction will
not harm it; if it is not sealed then it requires more reduction.
There are, of course, glazes inside the pots which are not going
to be affected by the salt because the lids are firmly sealed. These
glazes need reducing over a much longer period, so reduction con-
tinues also for their sake. I maintain a medium reduction until
the temperature is about 1240°C. At this point, glazes are melting,
the body is vitrifying hard, the silica is becoming active and salting
time is imminent.

I oxidize once again, because by now I know that the body is
sealing over and because by the time I get to 1260°C—1270°C
the body will be vitrified and any further oxidation is then less
likely to be beneficial. So I oxidize at 1260°C and the great mo-
ment comes when I start to salt. The salt has been dampened in
preparation and at 1260°C the clay is vitrifying, and at its best
for reaction with the salt. Salting usually takes about two hours,
though this depends very much on how much salt I have to put

into the kiln. This is governed by how much salt is left over from previous firings. In a new kiln the chamber has to be salted as well as the pots; this means that more salt has to be put in and salting takes longer. Bear in mind too that salt vapour causes the burners to perform less efficiently and a curtailing of temperature rise is almost inevitable until the kiln is oxidizing again. Salting usually takes about two hours and, provided that the process is not too rapid and the kiln has not dropped too much in temperature, by about 8.30 p.m. it should be completed. The kiln should still be at 1260°C–1270°C. At this point the atmosphere in the kiln is cleaned up by introducing more primary and secondary air and the temperature should begin to rise. The kiln is fired until about 1300°C. This is the point when, from previous experience, I know that the glazes are at their brightest. The reaction between body, slips and salt has been going on for about four or five hours and the rich textures and colours required have been achieved. This sometimes takes far longer than five hours. In my experience the longer this period is maintained the richer the results.

Salting procedure

There is no one method — salting can be done in any number of ways. I find the simplest way is to wrap the salt in paper packets, open the salt port above the burner and throw the packets in. Wrapped in paper 1 lb of salt makes a tennis ball-sized packet that can be very simply thrown into the kiln with the minimum amount of wastage and spillage. My method is to prepare the salt by dampening it — not wetting it: bear in mind here that wet salt thrown into the kiln creates steam. Too much steam will expand so rapidly that it will blow the door out of the kiln, so just dampen the salt enough to hold it together like a snowball.

For an average firing I prepare about 18 lbs of salt. With a new kiln 1 lb of salt will be needed for every cubic foot of kiln space. My kiln is about 40 cu. ft, so I started off with 40 lbs of salt and gradually, as the residual salt built up, reduced this amount. To prepare the kiln for salting I put the damper in the chimney half in, which restricts the pull of the chimney. This means that the exhaust gases cannot evacuate as efficiently and the burners begin to cause reduction. I therefore turn the

41

Fig. 4.4 *Opposite*: Here a test ring is being removed after the first salting has been done. The rings are arranged carefully in the kiln so that they can be extracted from time to time to show just how much salt the clay and ware have taken.
Photo: Homer Sykes.

burners down, so that they are again working at their optimum efficiency. Remember that by doing this it is difficult to keep the kiln temperature from falling. I then charge the kiln with about 2 lbs of salt, one packet of salt in front of each burner. This takes about five minutes to melt and I allow it to stay in the kiln for about ten minutes. After this I pull the damper out as the gases have by then done their work in the kiln. I then turn the burners up again for five minutes and repeat the cycle for as long as it takes to use up the amount of salt I have. Sometimes I put in more than 2 lbs of salt at a time, but this depends very much on how impatient I feel and if the temperature is such that I can afford to put in more than the minimum.

The only way of telling, apart from memory, experience and instinct, how much salt is actually being deposited on the pots is by using test rings. These small rings, about two inches in diameter and made of the same clay as the pots, are placed in strategic places by the spy holes in the door of the kiln. They are hooked out at intervals during the salting, and show how much glaze is forming on the pots. Reading these rings can only be learned by experience. The first ring is usually very dry, like a smooth sandpaper. Further rings go through stages of glassy, bobbly droplets. The final ring has a very glassy, very smooth surface in which every little mark and crease will show up clearly: even fingerprints left where the ring ends were joined together will show up distinctly. Another method of assessing the glaze is to put a metal rod into the kiln alongside a pot. The rod reflects on the wall of the pot and shows its degree of shine and its texture.

When I am satisfied that enough salt has been thrown in I remove the damper and turn the burners up. Since the kiln temperature will probably have been retarded, I raise it and then soak the kiln. This is simply a matter of sustaining the kiln at its high temperature, so that the chemical actions which take place at this temperature are prolonged. Chemical reactions that take place over a longer period give much more satisfactory results. When it has soaked enough I turn off the burners.

Cooling the kiln

When the kiln is soaking at these high temperatures, various forms of quartz develop in the body of the pots: some of this

quartz is very unstable, the most unstable form being cristobolite. As already mentioned, the more silica in the body, the
better it will salt. However, the more silica in the body, the
less chance there is of the pots staying in one piece when cooling. The most stable of these quartz forms is mullite which forms
if the kiln is cooled very rapidly. Instead of turning the kiln off,
turn the fuel off, but let the blowers keep blowing cold air into
the kiln and pull out all the bungs. The kiln temperature will
drop very rapidly allowing the formation of mullite and pre-
venting the formation of cristobolite. The pernicious effects of
excessive silica can therefore be stabilized by fast cooling the
kiln after the firing.

Fuming the kiln

This process takes place during the cooling cycle. It is a further
development of vaporizing the glaze with various metal oxides
in soluble salt form. These are vaporized and then passed through
the cooling kiln at around 750°C. At this temperature the glazes
are almost solidified on the pot. If, for example, stannous chloride
is introduced into the kiln the resulting vapours will roll through
the kiln and combine with the almost cool glaze to form
mother-of-pearl-like lustres on the sides of the pots. These qualities are particularly sympathetic to the salting process, rather than
the conventional way of applying lustres.

5 Clays, Glazes and Slips

Clays

Most clays may be salted with varying degrees of success. Some clays take a good coating of glaze while others reject the salt entirely. There is a close relationship between the silica content, iron content and temperature. The surface texture and colour of the glaze is a direct result of the firing technique employed and the composition of the clay body.

As a basic principle, the more silica in the clay the smoother the glaze will be, but with less silica, the more distinctive 'orange peel' texture will result. This broken surface derives from the dispersal of silica and alumina particles on the surface. The sodium fluxes the clusters of silica causing a covering of glass droplets to form. Obviously if insufficient silica is in the clay then a very dull surface will result. The brilliance of the glaze is governed by the silica content, and also by the temperature and the iron content of the clay. Iron has the effect of rejecting the salt; clays which otherwise would salt quite satisfactorily will not do so if the iron content is too high (obviously this characteristic can be used to advantage as a means of variegating the surface of a pot).

The formula of the clay body will give the potter a good idea of the results he is likely to expect from a salt kiln. The ratio of the silica to alumina, the iron content and the temperature of the firing are the most important things to note. Overleaf is listed a rough guide to the likely results from different formulae.

Silica	Alumina		
3	1	—	Distinct orange peel surface
4	1	—	Bright, smooth surface
5	1	—	Glassy surface, probably with minute crazing

iron content

1% FeO	—	Pale gold
1·5%	—	Pale tan
1·8—2%	—	Medium brown to dark brown
2—3%	—	Medium brown to black

Over 3% of iron causes the glaze to become progressively duller. Obviously the colour is governed as much by the nature of the firing as by the iron content. Traditionally, the saltglaze produced in England was oxidized, hence the preponderance of cream and buff-coloured ware. Therefore, should a clay which may contain too much iron for reduction be chosen, it may be used perfectly well under oxidizing conditions. The pale body colour may be desirable as it offers an interesting contrast with darker slips or glazes. The paleness of the clay can give greater clarity to the colours on its surface.

Traditionally, potters have tended to come to terms with the clay as they found it. However, today, as a result of modern technology almost an unlimited range of clays are available to us. An almost ideal clay body should therefore be obtainable by blending various clays together. Unfortunately, compromises have to be made in order to increase one component of the clay, for instance, the silica to facilitate salting and pernicious side effects may result. A clay, which in the vitrified matrix of the fired body will contain too much free silica, will almost certainly cause severe problems, most noticeably by shattering in the cooling cycle.

This may be remedied by increasing the alumina in the clay, thereby restoring a more stable balance, or by introducing, if possible, into the body an agent to encourage a more complete melt of the silica into the matrix. Felspar in small proportions can remedy this problem.

Composing a clay body is obviously a matter of compromise. This can, however, be less painful if slips of varying clays are employed. These can be applied to the pot to give a considerable range of colour and texture. Recipes for slips are included in subsequent chapters. White clays are most commonly used for salt bodies as an overall iron content of between 1% and 3% is desired. Ball clays and pale fire clays are most frequently chosen. The overall properties of the body is, of course, very much a matter of personal taste. Provided that the general guide lines listed are adhered to, a reasonable result will be achieved.

The use of ball clays or other fire clays may give a rather soapy clay which may need opening. Care should be taken with the choice of material used. Many grogs are made from iron bearing clay which may result in too heavy a speckle. Coarse sands often cause rough surfaces on rims, as the silica particle is too large to flux into the smooth surface of the clay, and remains as a protruberance, on edges in particular. Ideally, grog made from the body of the pot is the most suitable answer to the problem.

Recipes
1. Shiny Brown Slip
     50 Red Clay
     50 SM Ball clay

The red clay contains 9% iron oxide the ball clay 72% silica. The high iron and silica content gives the shiny dark surface.

2. Gold/tan slip. Semi-matt
     50% SMD Ball clay
     50   China Clay

The ball clay contains 1% iron oxide and 64% silica. The high alumina content of the china clay gives the semi-matt surface and a pink tinge to the colour.

3. Pink Slip
     66 Porcelain Clay
     33 China Clay

The high silica porcelain clay gives a bright surface and the high overall china clay content gives quite a bright pink colour. Heavy salting results in a lustrous surface.

4. Bright Orange Slip
   33 Porcelain Clay
   33 Potash Felspar
   33 CY or AT Ball clay

The orange colour derives from the iron in the CY clay (3·4%) reacting with the alumina in the clay 30%. The brightness comes from the silica in the porcelain and the felspar.

5. Semi-matt Orange Slip
   50 CY Ball clay
   50 Potash Felspar

CY clay is a low silica high alumina ball clay with 3% iron. In combination with equal parts of felspar a very attractive orange slip results.

Analysis of clays mentioned in recipes

	SiO_2	Al_2O_3	Fe_2O_3	
SMD Ball clay	67	21	0·92	
SM Ball clay	78	13	0·64	English China Clays Sales Co Ltd St. Austell Cornwall
AT(CY) Ball clay	52	30	2·6	
China Clay Cl	47·2	37·2	·70	Watts Blake and Bearne Newton Abbot, Devon

				Fluxes
Red Clay	62	27	7	4
Porcelain Body	72	22	0·7	5·3

The clays named in the recipes may not be available to many potters. If the above formulae code is compared with available clays a fair indication of their useability will be given.

Glazes

Glazes in the conventional sense are principally composed of silica which is a glass former. This is melted by adding fluxes to it, such as lead, whiting, magnesium, potash and sodiur etc, which reduce the temperature at which silica will melt, commensurate with the clay which is being used. In a salt kiln the fluxing is done by the sodium, therefore compounding a glaze for a salt kiln is really duplicating the action of the salt. The purpose of putting another clay surface on to the pot is to give variety and a further range of expression through different colours and textures. Most of the glazes used on a salt pot are in the form of a slip, in other words, they have a high proportion of clay in the recipe. This is particularly so in raw firing, for the more clay in the glaze or slip, the better it will adhere to the pot. The more siliceous the clay, the shinier the surface will be. The high alumina clays or those containing a high percentage of iron will give a very different surface to the pot. Dipping, spraying or painting these various slips on to the surface of the pot opens up a whole further range of decorative techniques. Textured surfaces can contrast with smooth ones, dry surfaces with 'wet'. Slips can be cut or wax resisted to reveal the body underneath. If a conventional glaze is used on a salt pot, further fluxes are added to a glaze which is already adequately fluxed, therefore the result cannot be anticipated. The additional flux may have a very dramatic effect on the colour of the glaze. If a very heavy iron glaze (which is usually dark brown or black) is used on a salt pot in a salt kiln, much of the iron is leached away. This results in a pale green glaze, which is far more fluid than it would be in an ordinary kiln. Basically, any clay can be used as a slip providing it can adhere to the pot. Slips can be used to vary the surface texture and colour of a pot without altering the basic body.

Some slips require a lot of salt in order to flux, while others require very little. The potter can work with, rather than against, his kiln by grouping slips with particular salt of temperature requirements in what he has found from experience to be appropriate areas of the kiln. For those kilns and shapes (such as deep bowls) which are consistently unpredictable in their capacity to salt, Shino type glazes offer a fairly good solution, as do low melting slips, such as American Albany, which form a glaze on their own. These offer one way of achieving an acceptable result whether the kiln has been kind to you or not, and they help reduce the seconds rate, which is usually high in a salt kiln.

Salt will not penetrate the inside of a covered or lidded pot so this can be glazed in the conventional way. Deep bowls present rather more of a problem, in that the gases tend not to pass to the

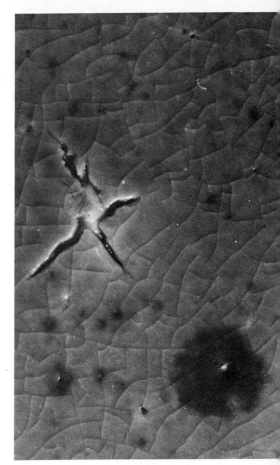

Fig. 5.1 Crazing. This happens during the cooling cycle. The hole in the centre of this photograph is an impurity in the clay. The brown marks are the result of iron particles.

49

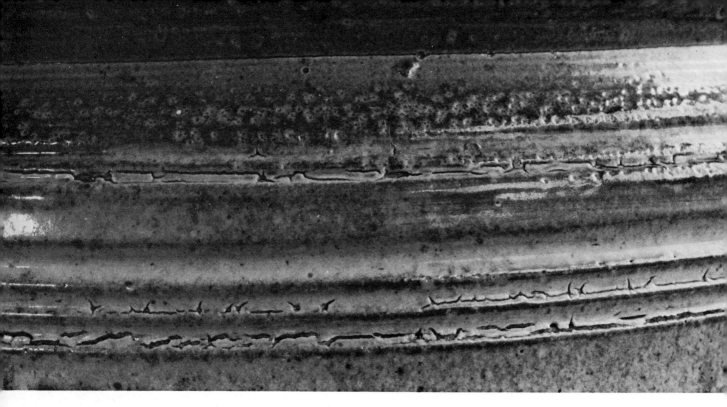

Fig. 5.2 *Above*: When slips are
used in place of glazes, difficulties
often occur with inconsistent
shrinkage. These problems can be
remedied by altering the plastic and
non-plastic elements in the recipe.
If the tolerance of the recipe does
not allow much alteration, calcining
plastic materials, e.g. ball clay, will
reduce the shrinkage. The introduc-
tion of clay into a glaze will help
adhesion to the raw clay body. Of
course biscuiting the pots greatly
adds to the range of slips and glazes
that can be used in a salt kiln.

Fig. 5.3 *Right*: Colander diameter
9 inches. See how the orange
peel effect is quite strong on the rim
but as you look further down into
the middle of this colander the
effect has died out as less salt vapour
reached it.

bottom of the pot but do affect the rim and a proportion of the inside. This particular problem can be solved by using a glaze which in itself fluxes sufficiently to be functional, while at the same time giving a good result with salt. Again Shino glazes are very useful.

Fig. 5.4 This is a close-up of the orange peel effect. This texture of orange peel is the surface most commonly associated with salt-glazing. It results from the uneven distribution of silica and alumina particles, which bring about a covering of droplets of glaze rather than the usual smooth coating of orthodox glazing. Obviously the more silica in the clay, the smoother the surface. Lower silica clays tend to have a more pronounced orange peel surface, though the quality of the glaze depends as much on the amount of salt which the pot receives as on the chemistry of the clay. Coarse sand also causes a knobbly surface.

Fig. 5.5 Salt vapour does not travel
easily inside vessels, consequently if
a smooth surface is required inside
the pots, then a lining must be
applied. As the upper part of the
inside will be affected by the salt,
this glaze should be tolerant to salt
if a moderately uniformed surface
is required. The amount of variation
tolerable is, of course, a matter of
personal taste. On the rim of this
jug the orange peel is very highly
defined, but the effect drops off
very quickly further down inside
the vessel.

Fig. 5.6 Lidded jar, height 15 inches. The recipe for the glaze at the top of this jar is as follows:

Recipe	Silica/Alumina ratio		Result
50 SMD Ball Clay	(63% SiO_2) (24% Al_2O_3)	silica and alumina almost	slip of medium brightness
50 China Clay	(24% SiO_2) (48% Al_2O_3)	equal	

The recipe for the bottom of this jar is as follows:

Recipe	Silica/Alumina ratio		Result
50 Felspar	(65% 6SiO_2) (17% Al_2O_3)	very high in silica	shiny glaze slight tendency to craze
50 China Clay	(24% SiO_2) (48% Al_2O_3)		

Fig. 5.7 Bread bin, height 15 inches. The recipe for the glaze at the top of this bin is as follows:

Recipe	Silica/Alumina ratio	Result
50 China Clay	$(24\% \; SiO_2$) $4 \; SiO_2$	orange coloured
	$(48\% \; Al_2O_3$) $3 \; Al_2O_3$	slip, fairly matt
50 A.T. Ball Clay	$(56\% \; SiO_2$)	
	$(24\% \; Al_2O_3$)	
	$(2 \cdot 5\% \; Fe_2O_3)$	

The recipe for the lower part of this bin is as follows:

Recipe	Silica/Alumina ratio	Result
50 China Clay	$(24\% \; SiO_2$) medium to	yellow/orange
	$(48\% \; Al_2O_3$) high silica,	slip, fairly
50 SM Ball Clay	$(72\% \; SiO_2$) iron and	bright. Rutile
	$(24\% \; Al_2O_3$) titanium	causing flecking,
25 CY Ball Clay	$(56\% \; SiO_2$) content	colour variation,
	$(24\% \; Al_2O_3$)	and extra fluidity
	$(2 \cdot 5\% \; Fe_2O_3)$	
5 Rutile	TiO_2	
	Fe_2O_3	

6 Packing a Salt Kiln

Packing a salt kiln is very much like packing an ordinary kiln in that the same basic rules apply: the pots should not be touching, and there should be a sufficient density of packing to give an even reduction and heat distribution. The difference is that in a salt kiln the vapour will glaze the whole of the interior as well as the pots: in order to prevent the pots and props sticking to the shelves and the lids sticking to the pots the potter must use an alumina resist. There are various ways of doing this. I find the simplest method is to mix alumina hydrate with water into a thin paste. This is painted around the rims of the lids or around the rims of the pots. All the shelves in the kiln are given a wash to prevent them adhering to the base of the ware.

Another method of separation is to use little pads, called wads, which are small button-sized lumps of alumina, china clay and possibly a little flour. The flour helps the non-plastic materials to stick together when handling. The wads are placed in between the lid and the pot, and on the base of the pot, so that it stands on three or four little pads of alumina. Patches of bare clay on the bases of salt pots indicate where the wads were placed. A good wad of alumina, or possibly a very refractory clay, placed in between the shelves and the props will prevent their sticking together. Cheap utilitarian wares, such as ginger beer bottles, wine jars or beer flagons, used to be piled into a kiln, fired and then prised apart with a crowbar. Many of these pots have quite distinct scars or bare patches where they were packed so closely that the salt vapour would not pass between them, but as they were made to be thrown away once used this did not matter. It is very interesting now to see one of these pots beautifully

Fig. **6.1** Wads on a rim. Wads are
pads of alumina and china clay
that are placed between the rim
and the lid before firing. These wads
can also be put at the base of the
pot and the shelf. The effects of
these are to stop the salt sealing
the surfaces together. Sufficient
wads should be used, particularly
on thin lids, otherwise the clay
may deform over the mound of
the wad. An alternative to wadding
is to paint the rims of the pots
with alumina. The shelves should
also be given a thick alumina wash.
A chamfer or a bevel at the base of
the pots again helps to prevent
adhesion. The alumina remaining
on the pots has to be removed by
rubbing with a carborundum stone,
which can be a very tedious business.

56

Fig. 6.2 This jar is typical of millions of cheap utilitarian pots that have been made all over Britain during the last three centuries. They were very roughly thrown, and are asymmetrical as you can see. They were all piled into the kiln, and salted. As they were little more than disposable household wares, very little care, or even thought, was given to the aesthetic effect the salt would have, and so you can see the variegating pattern on this body. There are all sorts of holes and flaws and at the top of the rim you can see where this pot has stuck to another and has been pulled apart, probably by knocking against something. This has left a very rough edge where the glaze has obviously stuck to the other pot.

Fig. 6.3 This is an old ink well. Its height is about 4 inches. You can see in the middle a mark where it stuck to the ink well next to it, during firing. If you look very closely to the right of the middle you can actually see a thumb print on the body.

salted on one side and badly scarred on the other. It is a Western idiosyncrasy to prize technical perfection more than aesthetic considerations: the one per cent of blemish somehow negates the 99 per cent of good points to enjoy in a pot. The whole Stoke-on-Trent pottery industry is based on this principle of seconds and slightly sub-standard ware and the costing factor revolves around it.

The 'setting up' of the kiln is all important i.e. the encouraging of things to happen by pre-empting the behaviour of the kiln and using the forces of flame pattern, vapour pattern, variations of heat which are known from past experience. The potter must be aware of the strengths or weaknesses of different areas in the kiln and adapt his pots, glazes and slips accordingly. If a kiln is packed more or less the same way for each firing then results are moderately predictable.

If the kiln is packed very densely the vapour will not reach every part of the kiln setting. It will find its way out through the easiest exit, by-passing some pots altogether, particularly those in the centre of the setting. The pots on the outside of the shelf may be well glazed, while those on the inside are not glazed at all. This is particularly likely to happen if the pots are packed very close to the shelf above, restricting the passage of the vapour still further. Again, if there is a lot of variation between large pots and small ones, the salt vapour will tend to find the easiest way out and the spaces around very big pots will get more salt and the denser pack of small pots will be by-passed altogether. As with any other kiln the denser the packing the more likely the kiln is to reduce evenly throughout. A loose pack tends to make for a slightly better salting in that there is a very good circulation and dispersal of vapours.

Once you know how your kiln works, you can exploit its firing characteristics. Interesting effects can be obtained by encouraging the patterns of salt and flames in a specific direction. For instance, the ware on the open side of the setting will receive a lot of salt and the chemical reaction on that side of the pots will be very different from that on the side which receives less salt. The resulting colour variations will be individual to each piece.

Three basic objectives when using a salt kiln are to pack the kiln as economically as possible, to encourage a good circulation of flame and salt, to give an even salting, and to maintain evenness of temperature unless very tolerant clays and glazes are being used.

Fig. 6.4 Jane Hamlyn's kiln packed and ready for the door to be bricked in. You can see how the pots have, in some cases, been carefully placed to make sure of producing attractive setting up.

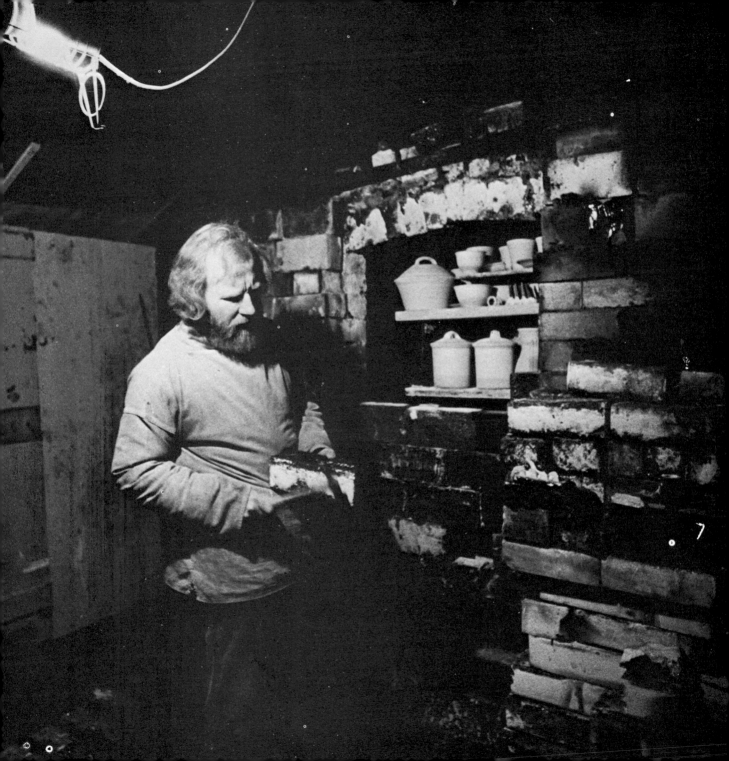

Space should be left in front of spyholes for withdrawing the test rings which should be placed in plenty, preferably at the top and bottom of the setting. If possible, some should also be placed at the front and back of the kiln. The test rings are withdrawn during salting to show the build-up of salt in the kiln. They are really the only guide to how the firing is progressing. Pyrometric sheaths will be attacked by the salt and are expensive. They can be protected to some extent by alumina or perhaps by a shield, such as a hollow kiln prop, but in this case they may read rather inaccurately. Pyrometric cones can be used with, or instead of, a pyrometer. Cones tend to be inaccurate once they have been salted since they are made of the same materials as glazes. When salted they flux and tend to bend rather sooner than their denoted temperature. They are only a rough guide once salting has started. They are, however, very useful in indicating when to salt. When I fire, I watch the cones up to 1260°C and salt at this temperature. As long as I have the same make of cones which I know melt at a certain temperature, even though the kiln may not actually be at 1260°C, I know from previous experience that I have a constant.

Salting is about building up your own experience. I could fire another potter's kiln and make a complete mess of it because it is so personal and delicate a process. So, the cones are really only an approximation until you have actually salted a kiln, after that an intelligent reading of the rings, particularly after you have salted and during the soaking of the kiln, will give a better guide to what is happening in the kiln itself. When salting, the rings indicate how much salt to put in; later, when soaking the kiln, they show how smoothly the glazes are fluxing out and give some idea of the way the temperature is climbing in the kiln. Beyond that you have to rely on instinct and your own experience.

There are ways in which you can encourage certain special effects. Sometimes they work, sometimes they don't and sometimes they are overdone, but salting is an enthusiast's game: you have to delight in what you are doing. You have to be slightly crazy to want to do this anyway. You are destroying your kiln every time you fire it. You are risking your pots. You are actually indulging in a medium that you do not really understand and, what is more, you do not want to understand because that way you would lose the magic. So, some of the special effects aimed for may seem rather bizarre to a more conventional potter.

Fig. 6.5 *Opposite*: Bricking up the kiln door. You can see the test rings and cones on the shelf. A spy will be right next to these.
Photo: Homer Sykes.

Fig. **6.6** The interminable wait. 'You are in a tense situation outside the kiln and all you can trust in is your ability to fire the kiln, your ability to understand the kiln from your previous experience and your ability to *understand* what fire does to pots. This is a very tantalizing situation, particularly when many weeks' work can be ruined in a matter of moments. One wrong decision at a given time when you haven't read what's happening correctly, you haven't got the experience, or your instinct lets you down . . . .'
Photo: Homer Sykes.

The most striking can be achieved by introducing additional materials, such as soluble salts of metal oxides in the kiln. In a conventional kiln, copper fired in an oxidizing atmosphere will give green pots; if fired in a reducing atmosphere it will give blood red pots. Copper sulphate introduced into a salt kiln will evaporate together with the salt. Copper and sodium vapour pass through the kiln together glazing everything a bright blood red. The result of this is that the next firing will again give a blood red to everything. Cobalt, in its soluble form, turns everything blue. Copper and cobalt used together give the most dramatic red, white and blue pots: the clay will be whitish, the cobalt will give blue, and the copper will give red. This happens in the first firing: on the second firing there will be a residue in the kiln already, so the results will not be quite the same. After several firings the effect will be lost altogether.

Although each firing gives different effects the results of these methods may be a little overwhelming. One or two red pots, for example, may be quite nice, but a whole kiln full of them will be too much of a good thing. It is possible, however, to restrict the effect by localizing the areas of copper in the kiln. The simplest way of doing this is to place a piece of copper, a coin will do, in a small cup or container on a shelf next to a pot. When this melts in the firing it will be fluxed by the salt and a small amount of volatilized copper will waft its way around the nearest pots giving the slightest hint of a pink blush. On porcelain or on a pale coloured body this is particularly attractive. Alternatively, a prop next to a certain pot could be painted with either cobalt or copper. Copper can also, of course, be painted directly on to the pot, but this eliminates the element of chance which is the great attraction of the other methods. Another way of introducing variables is to put a metal object, such as a beer can, in the firebox. Beer cans have a thin coating of tin, which is an opacifying glaze giving an element of whiteness. However, at very high temperatures tin, when fluxed with sodium, gives the pots a slightly pearly effect. Since tin is very expensive, you are unlikely to be able to throw in cupfuls of tin oxide, but you can throw in the odd can, and there is probably enough tin on a beer can to give a pearly effect on the pots closest to it. Similarly, old copper nails, brass nuts and bolts will give off enough copper to make an interesting surface.

Essentially what I'm talking about here is enjoying yourself.

If you don't enjoy the excitement of the firing, you don't enjoy the anticipation of it, and really anticipation is what it's all about. There are all kinds of other ways to get special effects. Banana skins draped over the necks of the pots reduce to an ash in firing and help flux the surface of the pots in addition to the salt. If you are lucky you may have shadow areas where the skin rested on the pot. If you soak the banana skin, an apple or orange peel or an old piece of cloth in cobalt, copper or nickel or anything else which will alter the surface and the colour of it, it will burn off, leaving the ash, and will help to flux the chemical which is saturated in it. The Japanese have a very nice method of soaking straw rope in brine, so that it absorbs salt, They wrap this round the pot and tie it up in a knot; when fired the rope burns away, and the salt impregnates the pot together with the ash and the rope, leaving rope patterns over the otherwise bare clay. You can dream up a whole range of these special effects for yourself.

7 Pollution and Safety

The effluent of a salt kiln is principally composed of dilute hydrochloric acid, chlorine gas and carbon monoxide. While this must obviously be respected as a lethal mixture, sensible precautions can prevent its causing any actual damage. Good ventilation both of the kiln and the kiln shed is essential. The kiln should have a tall chimney to encourage good evacuation of vapour with sufficient velocity to project it twenty feet into the atmosphere. On a reasonably fine breezy day, the vapour will be quickly dispersed. Firing should not take place on a damp, still day because the hydrochloric vapours will combine with the water in the atmosphere and settle as a kind of smog over the area of the kiln. The kiln must be sited out of doors; however well ventilated a room is, there will still be a considerable amount of dangerous vapour in the air and this will cause sickness if inhaled over a long period.

Metal of any kind is very badly corroded by salt. If possible the kiln chimney should be built of brick rather than metal tube, and the iron work of the kiln should be protected with a good aluminium paint (which obviously contains alumina) so that it is not corroded. The tiebars which support the arch can be very quickly eaten through and present a serious danger if they weaken during the firing, when the kiln is under quite high tension. Besides this, the metal parts of buildings, or even vehicles in the area of the kiln can be damaged if they are heavily salted-up over a long period. The obviously anti-social aspects of saltglazing must be borne in mind.

There is not really a great deal you can do about salt vapour coming from the kiln unless you salt with another material, such as borax, which gives a similar effect but has the advantage of not giving off toxic fumes. In many areas where clean air zones exist by law, saltglazing is probably illegal, and before building a salt kiln, the approval of the local authority should be obtained. One way of avoiding being a nuisance is to salt at night when less people are going to be inconvenienced by their own private fog!

As stated earlier, the chimney design is particularly important in a salt kiln which has, in effect, to evacuate twice as much vaporous refuse as a conventional kiln. In order to give a good velocity to the gases so that they are pushed out into the atmosphere as high as possible, 50 per cent more height should be added to the chimney and it should be tapered so that the reducing volume of gases fit a reducing diameter of chimney and the velocity is maintained. Cowls, which are often introduced to stop back pressure in kilns, should be avoided if possible because they tend to restrict and to baffle the salt fumes as they leave. However, there are various methods by which the gases can be diluted before they actually leave the chamber itself. If cold air is introduced to the salt vapours after they have done their work in the kiln chamber, it will help dilute them before they actually pass through the chimney itself. The simplest way to introduce cold air into a chimney is to remove a brick, but this has the same effect as introducing a damper, for by forcing cold air into the chimney the pull is reduced.

Once the vapours pass under the floor of the kiln, they are no longer any use to the pots and therefore the first place to introduce a port is beneath the floor into the flue directly below the shelves. This can be done very simply on a down-draught kiln, as shown in Fig. 3.8 on page 25, with a loose brick in the front of the kiln underneath the door. When this is removed cold air is sucked directly underneath the floor of the kiln itself and immediately dilutes the gases. At the same time, of course, the pull on the chimney is reduced; the damper should therefore be opened fully so that the chimney is pulling from its base to its maximum extent, but is not evacuating the fumes from the chamber before they have actually worked on the pots. A long horizontal flue between the back wall of the kiln and the chimney base can also be useful in that bricks can be removed along this area. Alternatively, baffles (a series of bricks) can be introduced in this flue in order to reduce the velocity of the fumes, bearing in mind, of course, the minimum amount of pull necessary to fire the kiln.

Fig. 7.1 The art of coarse potting. Filling the elevated tank which feeds the burners by gravity. This tank was bought cheaply from a vehicle crash yard. It was brand new and had been made too big for the truck and therefore sold off cheap! It holds 40 gallons and is absolutely ideal for use, as here. You can see how far the kiln is from any other building, and how rudimentary the kiln shed is. Photo: Homer Sykes.

8 Conclusion

What I like about salting is its drama. You are an alchemist, you know the chemistry but you also retain to some extent the magic, because the chemistry is incomplete and there are so many variables. Besides this, of course, you are working with the basic elements of earth (clay), fire and water. With a simple handful of salt you have the power to transform the pots in the kiln into something unique and wonderful. You have the power to wreck it all too. You are outside and the pots are inside at 1300°C. They are so hot you cannot even look at them. You are striking a very fine balance between being master of the kiln and its slave. It is a fascinating and all-embracing situation which no other form of making, for me anyway, can match.

The unpredictability of it all makes unpacking the kiln even more exciting. You can't get the door off fast enough to see what has happened, and of course at white hot temperatures a good firing and a bad firing look much the same. You just don't know what is in there: you feel incredible elation if it's right and acute depression if it's wrong, but what you always have is the wish to get on the wheel, make some more and do it again, if only to rectify mistakes or to capitalize on a new triumph. The best pot is the next pot, the best firing is going to be the next one. Because if you are clever enough you have learned from the last one. If half a dozen people, using exactly the same materials, fire their kilns in exactly the same way, there will be a different pot from each kiln, because the flames never touch a pot in the same way: every pot is unique. Each firing is a new and different experience and this is what I find so attractive about saltglazing.

Fig. 8.1 Leaching on a hard edge. Edges of handles and rims, or any sharp articulation, will be more viciously attacked by the salt. As salting bodies are low in iron, this action by the salt results in pale edges showing through the darker surface. Because of this characteristic, indentations of incising, scratching and sprigging have been extensively used as a means of exploiting the possibility of textural decoration. Any texture shows in sharp relief, offering unlimited scope for decoration.

72

Fig. 8.2 *Left*: The top of a lidded jar showing leaching, the highly decorative orange peel, and on the right in the reflection the very shiny glaze effect.

Fig. 8.3 *Above*: A covered box, height 4 inches. See how the colour goes from dark at the top, to light at the bottom, due to more salting at the top.

Fig. 8.4 *Overleaf*: A jug by Jane Hamlyn.

Fig. 8.5 *Overleaf opposite*: Casserole, height 9 inches.

Fig. 8.6 *Left*: A porcelain pot by
Jane Hamlyn.

Fig. 8.7 *Above*: Lidded jar, height
16 inches. This shows the body of
the jar, the top is shown in Fig. 8.2.

Fig. 8.8 *Far left*: Storage jar, height 10 inches.

Fig. 8.9 *Left*: A colander by Jane Hamlyn.

Fig. 8.10 *Above*: Simple salted table ware.

Fig. 8.11 *Right*: Two pots by Walter Keeler.

Epilogue

The previous chapters of the book have been principally concerned with the methods of saltglazing. I should like to consider how, and perhaps why, these techniques might be used.

The obvious reason for saltglazing is, of course, to achieve the particular qualities of texture, colour and surface which no other technique can give. The approach adopted in making pots for salt is fundamentally different, in one vital respect, from conventional techniques. Because the glazing is achieved during the firing and in a large part comes from the pot itself, the potter must in his mind's eye maintain an image of the anticipated surface he hopes to attain. Saltglazing is a revealing process. The surface of the clay is not coated with the glaze as in other techniques, but the surface qualities are emphasized by the brightening of the resulting glaze. The pot returns from the kiln close to its state when freshly formed. This factor demands perhaps a greater emphasis on the initial methods of making and their consequent surface detail.

We have only to look at the work of saltglazers in the past to understand this approach. Dwight's portrait of his daughter Lydia is a beautiful example of the clarity of detail which salting achieves. No mark made on the clay has been lost. The result is a cool, almost marble-like surface, so very different from the more robust, flamboyant textures of the bellarmine makers whose rich 'orange-peel' surfaces have awakened interest in so many potters. Between the work of the English creamware period and the modern studio potter is a wealth of variety, not only of colour and texture, but of form, usage and even status. It is interesting that the technique has been used for portraits of kings and the making of sewer pipes! What these seemingly distant cousins have in common is that the potter chose that technique to give the particular surface only salt could give. It is an interesting aspect of salting that although its usage has fluctuated between the grandiose and the humble, the methods employed over several years have still left for today's salter, a wealth of opportunity for developing the technique.

For me, one of the most exciting aspects of salting is that new standards can be achieved and that past attainment can be a starting point, rather than a hallowed criterion which can only be approached rather than emulated. This is not to say, however, that precious achievements are easily surpassed, indeed while the technology may be attained, perhaps the 'complete pot' may prove somewhat more elusive. As with other techniques, asethetic development often comes with technological advancement. Since the demise of salting as an industrial method, the achieving of new standards in salting is perhaps more in the hands of the studio potter, than it is with other methods. Salting in itself is beautifully simple, deceptively so, but is still open to infinite exploration. Bernard Leach's *Toward a Standard* instances the Sung period of Chinese ceramics as a touchstone of quality. To me no such period commands quite the same attention in the field of saltglazing, although this is a very personal matter. Today, what is good 'salting' is a very open question. I consider this to be a very healthy and invigorating situation as it requires the potters themselves to set the standards and bring into play those sensibilities, which perhaps have been allowed to become dormant, in consideration of more conventionally made ceramics.

As a result of this, a saltglazing potter may find himself rather isolated (not just because of the fumes), but because of the loneliness involved in any pioneering enterprise. The wrong turnings and pitfalls are legion. There is no easy solution to be found on the bookshelf, or in the technical journal: he must draw his own conclusions from a course of action, and rely on building-up a store of experience while developing instincts, in progressing towards the elusive realization of that image of the quality he hopes to achieve.

Salting requires a particular mentality — the ability to step into the unknown and to risk everything in order to advance. For many potters, firing is an annoying but necessary inevitability, often to be completed with the minimum of fuss and the maximum predictability — nothing could be further from the saltglazer's attitude to his kiln. To him his kiln is the vehicle between his anticipations and his realizations but at times it is an instrument of wilful caprice, often exerting a life of its own, resulting in undeserved reward or uncalled for rebuttal. This approach is, of course, a romantic one bound up, as it is, with the element of fire; as Paracelsus put it, 'What is accomplished by fire is alchemy, whether in the furnace or kitchen stove'.

Appendix 1 Suppliers list

UK suppliers

Clays, glazes and pottery supplies

Podmore and Son Ltd., Shelton, Stoke, Staffs. 0782 24571.

Potclays Ltd., Brickkiln Lane, Etruria, Stoke, Staffs. 0782 29816.

Harrison Mayer Ltd., Meir, Stoke, Staffs. 0782 31611.

The Fulham Pottery Ltd., 210 New King's Road, London, SW6. 01 736 1188.

Ferro (GB) Ltd., Wombourne, Wolverhampton, Staffs. 09077 4144.

Wengers Ltd., Etruria, Stoke, Staffs. 0782 25126.

Bricks and castables

Gibbons Refractories Ltd., P O Box 19, Dudley, W. Midlands. 0384 53251.

Morganite Refractories Ltd., Neston, Wirral, Cheshire. 051 336 3911

Silbond Refractories Ltd., Herries Road, Sheffield 6. 1742 348074.

Kilns and Furnaces Ltd., Keele St Works, Tunstall, Stoke, Staffs. 0782 84642.

Fire Gas Kilns Ltd., Newstead Trading Estate, Trentham, Stoke, Staffs. 0782 23641.

Wheels

J W Ratcliffe and Sons, Old Boro Works, Rope St., Shelton New Rd., Stoke. 0782 611321.

Ceramic fibre
Fiberfrax Carborundum, Carborundum & Co Ltd., Mill Lane,
   Rainford, St Helens, Lancs. 074 488 2941.

Oil burners
Auto combustion, Harcourt, Halesfield 13, Telford, Salop.
   0952 585574.
Nu-way Air and Gas Mixers, P O Box 14, Berry Hill, Droitwich,
   Worcs. 09057 4244.

Oil kilns
Midland Monolithic Furnace Lining Co. Ltd., Barwell, Leics.
   0455 42061.

Gas kilns and installations
Bricesco Kilns, Bricesco House, Park Ave., Woolstanton,
   Newcastle-under-Lyme, Staffs.

US suppliers

Burners and parts
Flynn Burner Corp., 425 Fifth Ave., New Rochelle, N.Y. 10802.
Johnson Gas Appliance Co., Cedar Rapids, Iowa 52405.
Maxon Corp., 201 E. 18th St., Muncie, Ind. 47302.
Mine & Smelter Industries (formerly DFC Corp.) P O Box 16607,
   Denver, Colo. 80216
Pyronics Inc., 17700 Miles Ave., Cleveland, Ohio 44128
Ransome Gas Industries Inc., 2050 Farallon Drive, San Leandro,
   Calif. 94577

Pottery material suppliers
American Art Clay Co. Inc., 4717 W. 16th St., Indianapolis,
   Ind. 46222.
Cedar Heights Clay Co., 50 Portsmouth Road, Oak Hill, Ohio
   45656.
Creek Turn Pottery Supply, Route 38, Hainesport, N.J. 08036.
A. P. Green Co., 1018 E. Breckenridge St., Mexico, Mo. 65265.
Hammill & Gillespie Inc., 225 Broadway, New York, N.Y. 10007.

Minnesota Clay, 8001 Grand Ave. So., Bloomington, Minn. 55420.

The Monomy Potter's Supply Co., RFD 140E, Chatham, Mass. 02633.

Newton Potters Supply Inc., 96 Rumford Ave., Box 96, Newton, Mass. 02165.

Rovin Ceramics and Pottery, 6912 Schaefer Road, Dearborn, Mich. 48216.

The Salem Craftsmen's Guild, 3 Alvin Pl., Upper Montclair, N.J. 07043.

Standard Ceramic Supply Co., Box 4435, Pittsburgh, Pa. 15205.

Trinity Ceramic Supply Co., 9016 Diplomacy Row, Dallas, Texas 75235.

Van Howe Co., 1185 S. Cherokee Avenue, Denver, Colo. 80223.

Westwood Ceramic Supply Co., 14400 Lomitas Avenue, City of Industry, Calif. 91744.

Refractory suppliers

Babcock & Wilcox Co., Refractories Div., 161 E. 42 Street, New York, N.Y. 10017.

A. P. Green Co., 1018 E. Breckenridge Street, Mexico, Mo. 65265.

Carborundum Co., Refractories and Electronic Div., Box 337, Niagara Falls, N.Y. 14302.

Denver Fire Clay Co., 2401 E. 40th Avenue, Box 5507, Denver, Colo. 80217.

Grefco Inc., 299 Park Avenue, New York, N.Y. 10017.

Metropolitan Refractories, Tidewater Terminal, So. Kearney, N.J. 07032.

New Castle Refractories, Box 471, New Castle, Pa. 16103.

Norton Co., Industrial Ceramics Division, Worcester, Mass. 01606.

Pyro Engineering Corp., 200 S. Palm Avenue, Alhambra, Calif. 91801.

Appendix 2 Bibliography

Notes on the Use of Borax in Saltglazing — Borax Consolidated 1948.

Staffordshire Saltglazed Stoneware — A. R. Mountford (Barrie & Jenkins), 1971.

The A.B.C. of English Saltglaze Stoneware — J. F. Blacker (Stanley Paul & Co. London), 1922.

Kilns — Daniel Rhodes (Chilton, Philadelphia, 1968; Pitman, London, 1969).

Pioneer Pottery — M. Cardew (Longmans, Harlow, Essex, 1969; St. Martin's, New York, 1971).

Saltglazing — Don Reitz (American Crafts Council), 1970.

Index